Soul of Poe

I0159494

By T.A. Starks

STLLC/Signs & Symbols Publishing

Cover art by: Erinn Campbell

COPYRIGHT 2016
ISBN: 978-0-9963556-5-0

Savage Life

Cold nights, clutching the cold pipe

Under the street lights

Squatting on cold stairs

With a hand out receiving cold stares

For a handout

-

Cold hearted pedestrians scurry by

Arms covered with tracks

Her family searches for her

But she covers her tracks

As she secretly works the tract

-

On her back she will lay

In the cockpits of Cadillac's for crack

Daddy's little girl no more

Occasionally a whore

But who's keeping track or score?

-

She is

-

In and out of centers trying to find her center

She wants to escape

But the white flakes soft and hard grips

Chapped lips wrap around main veins

Just so that she can maintain without the shakes

"For God's Sake," she prays, "My soul to take."

Mable

Bathed in the blue screen light of my television

As shadows from random objects loom on my cell walls

A low fan hums in a neighboring cell

Providing me with a strange comfort

-

Sealed eyes with moist corners

My mind cascades like molting snowy owl feathers on a
Northern wind

As my spirit transcends and travels on an unworldly plane

The spiritual

-

Outside my physical while she sleeps

My mother I keep

Closer than she'll ever know

Not Black not White

And do they kill at will or at the will of the ruler?

With all power don't we see that nothing slips by he?

Almighty...

-

Alrighty

Send the man on dark night into the picture show

While the dark night plays

And so walk did he with McVeigh

Still...

-

Yet we marvel at the miracles of childbirth

And deaths close calls

But not at all his horrid plans

Which he commands before man

-

After school registrations

Mass annihilations

The children's souls ascend to the kingdom with reservations

And without the rise of the ladder

-

Yet we do marvel at the winder breeze and summer trees

And state: "God is good all the time, and all the time God is good!"

Confession Room

In my current situation

Most of the time I just want to give up the ghost

Like the son

-

In my current position

Most of the time I just want to forever leave this post

But fear the beyond

-

Oh the salty liquid building inside my ducts

The quivering illness, which is my sadness

Release the body's water heated flux

The shivering rage, which is my madness

-

In my current tribulation

I am ready but not ready to release my fears

Because I cannot swim

-

Nor can I steer an uncontrollable boat afloat

In my tears

Her Life's, His Life's Goal

Daddy, daddy, I can't sleep

Tears she shed from under the sheet

Coo and comfort he rubs her head

Then checks for monsters under the bed

-

Reassured in her daddy's cradle

Her fear melts, now safe and stable

But daddy has worries and it lies in his arms

She is his fear

When growing with charm

Circle of Life

Pink folds of flesh

Guards the gateway

To man's ultimate quest

Which is her eggs expected guest

Solely

Fist to chin I ponder like Rome's famous statue

My mind floats back to the days of old

My youth

Unfold the truth through these eyes of proof

Remains burned on my cranial roof

-

Seven souls kindred, lodged, governed by a tyrant bipolar

Our mother's birther

Back then bound by sad circumstances

We clung to each other like ticks

While taking our mental licks

-

Hearts transfixed on the brighter days promised

Fast forward through the years of oppression

Simulating curiosity to rebellion of man's law landing

One in a prison state

Me

-

Sentenced to a 40 year castrate

Now I wonder like Stevie in the darkness

Behind my eyelids on the edge of self-destruction

I search for where our broken connection lies

Tracking back through time

But cannot find

-

My kinder cousin's release

"Out of sight, out of mind…"

Never disregard our ties that bind

Reflection

I know why the caged bird sings...

Sing; sing birdman me incarcerated like a circus bear

Only my roar is a life melody

-

Formulated with thoughts and deep rooted emotions from my soul...

Manifested through songs and poems

To ease my mental state

To keep my mental demons at bay

While my body rots away

-

Sold my life for a night crime

And in a night's time

I was sentenced to what seems to be a lifetime

-

Now I time life perched up top my bunk

Watching the sun go up and down

Making way for the moon to do the same

-

Oh I know why it sings

It sings because it has to

Otherwise it will be mute

And that's not a bird's way

Birdman me it is not my way

That's why I know

Frankly Speaking

I was a coward and I pray forgiveness with palms up

Now I return to the time in 1999

I remember seeing him coming

Dressed in tan from shirt to slacks

An ode to the 80's with an uncanny facial likeness and smile

Which made me mimic only with sadness behind mine

-

Dusty he was

But we conversed on grandma's porch

On the most beautiful day

And in that time he was whole and mind went not astray

Once, maybe...

-

A great man was he before the shaya'teen whispered the
wonders of butter

Colored pebbles that burned away the problems

A great man?

I can't say...

Hell, she thought enough to play

Lay and birth a babe

-

But they beat him through, chased him down and on the ground

Laid hands and feet to his body meat

And spit and cursed him for something he said to a rat of the hood

-

Many secretly knew her in backwoods and seats

About this I was told and I laughed and laughed

Until I was away from the "cool kids"

Then I hung my head, gripping temples in shame

And buried it within for 15 years

Never speaking his name

On a Street Hustlers Wife No. 1
Sprung

Locked eyes of love

Glamorous life she wanted as much

Willing to give it up

Her virtue untouched

-

A roll in the hay

Many times a day

In love-lust with danger she would stay

On a Street Hustlers Wife No. 2
A Union

On the edge of hope for him in changing

Acceptance of his golden ring brings marriage

-

Happiness bring bliss

In the form of an infant carriage

-

Educational dreams on hold

As warning signs unfold

-

With unanswered "hellos" on the line

She would inquire as much

But he's in the streets all the time

Force Feed Them Truths

Took them from their homes packed and stacked below the deck

Where even death grimaced working

Chattled human cattle

The Jones raise their paddles on Plymouth select for stock and breed

-

300 plus

In slavers cuffs

Singing spirituals to ease

Bullwhip lashes while tied to trees

-

Stained cotton by the tons pack rag dolls for their young

Who play with blood, sweat, and tears

Clothed with the same

Washed brains

The West holds no shame

-

They'll never make that Dred Scott change

¾ a human still remains

From whence they came they'll never proclaim

Trace the line and you will find

That only one original race can create all others

-

Show me a Caucasian couple who birthed an African child

And I'll show you a man who can walk on the surface of the sun

All roads lead past Rome to the one history books do not provide

But hide the truth

Unable to deny the proof

That connects every human being to the roots

Words on the Wind for Open Hearts

There, a pain in my heart

Can you see it?

At dusk, just after the sun goes down

And the orange glow of the street lamps buzz on

Can you see it?

-

As the rising and falling sound of the locust cry

Can you feel my pain?

Mmm...I smell it... Summer

Barbecue, fresh cut grass, tell me

Can you even grasp the thought of being alone?

-

Being disowned while the world dances on

I just want to be free

But the system won't release me

Not until my time...2039!

Three years before 59 for the crimes I committed

-

But change I am committed

So I use my time wisely

Like Nelson and Little, doing my best

To solve life's riddles

-

On the yard I walk my thoughts of life beyond the gates

And I smile at the strangest things like

A simple picnic by the stream while the surface gleams

Or a mid-day nap on a king while Anita Baker sings

-

But there's a pain in my heart and it is unmendable

Until I break the chains and regain my freedom

Until then...

When the locusts cry on a warm summer evening

Know that miles away I wonder if

You are wondering if I'm wondering

A Hunger For?

Many things on my mind

Locked down doing time

Waiting to exhale like

Loretta Devine

-

I wonder do they think about me

The women of my past what about me do they ask?

In knots my stomach twist

Thinking on the ifs makes me sad

Just wondering

-

One woman for sure cried

My mother who loves this man

So I wonder, did old flames burn in mourning?

Being also female born

Did any care enough to do so?

-

From them

For me I find myself wanting that

And if only one did it would make me feel

Honored with bliss

The truth never tell me

And let me please have the tears

Serenity

Standing with me, myself, and I

Some place, any place

Far away

-

The sun beaming down on my brown flesh

The cool fresh smog-less air massaging my lungs

-

Maybe I'll sit on the grass

As soothing as a bubble bath

Soft as cotton so inviting just for me

-

Maybe I'll just stroll the forest and take in the sights

And watch the animals live their lives

Climb a mountain

And camp out under the sky

-

Smile at the constellations

So high and speak with my creator

With the moment as my theater

-

"Father…master of the universe…

Thank you for my serenity

Thank you for my inner peace."

On a Street Hustlers Wife No. 3
Stagnated

In love with a snake

Body covered in bites

At home with the seeds alone every night

-

Moon stage has taken its flight

Leaving a tormented heart in plight

-

Now

Hasty actions make her wonder

Reconsidering her blunder a plan

To hatch to come from under

On a Street Hustlers Wife No. 4
The Escapist

Used...

The magic dissipated with abuse administered

-

Dreams...

The vision to pixilated with hopes so castrated

Locked eyes of hate

An ugly life she could never want

Her mother's premonition

Haunts as she contemplates what to take

-

In stealth

Ushering the kids out

To the nearest bus route

The Holideck

Hand my presidential ID to the doorman

Who scans it to make sure it's real

I'm so happy I'm shaking with pain to ender the Holideck field

-

And so I carry my bags in each hand

To my room which is dark as the night

It's okay, I flick the bic and unpack my bags for the flight

-

I strap in and so it begins

Inhale deep as I plug in the jack

Destinations what you imagine just like it is on Star Trek

-

The room transforms to a place I love

A zone where I dance and dance

The Holideck's my saving grace

From the real world in which I feel banned

-

And so I keep coming back day after day after day

Chasing after that very first ride

Oh how I wish I could stay

Sacred Time

My casa I enter and shed all business garments

With haste I gather things needed

And set them accordingly

-

One flute crystal filled with chilled grapes

Liquid from the good year of my birth

1978

-

Hot water laced with beads

That bloom into clouds that fizzle which tickles

While waxy sticks burn illuminating the once was now turned
sanctuary of tranquility

-

With a low glow

Dip a toe

In I go

-

Submerged now in wet wonder

Exhale now gay as Stevie Wonder in tones "A Ribbon in the Sky"

Grooves my soul

-

Inhale deeply the scent of lavender enters my nose

Relaxation

Now ajar my curvy stilts invite digits middle and ring

To slowly provoke my bulb to relinquish dopamine throughout
my being

-

Oculars roll to whites and close with licked lips

That soon are bottom bitten

Now ingress the temple with fingers stated balmy polishing
walls

Piston motions slow, but growing

Worldly tensions out-flowing as I remain rowing

-

Oh how the fruition makes me whisper

Self-praise escapes my watering mouth

That time is almost about as shockwaves curl my toes

To cracking and I can't help but moan

"It's happening."

In The darkness

Lying in my bunk last night in the darkness

Trying to find my way home

My thirst for freedom can't be quenched

By the coldest spring water

\-

Nor can my hunger for love be killed

By the hardest meal

Locked down behind bars and barbed wire fences

Secluded from the outside world

The world which olds everything I know

\-

Now is truly dear

So packed with sadness

That my eyes leak unwanted tears

But on one will ever know this true pain

\-

But this darkness

My friend darkness

Nonjudgmental

Always listening

Always there

Always

The Sale, the Cycle

The last bag should go for ten

But he'll take a fin

He want to go in

-

The fiend comes and buys the rock

Runs off the block

She's on the clock

-

Back at the spot she can hardly wait

As she readied the pipe to smoke the bait

Dopes good, too good to slow so she post to Hoe to buy some more

-

A John comes and she hops right in and degrades herself for only a ten

But wait

Johns a fake

-

He doesn't want her to leave and so he rapes

Shame

And it's all a part of the game

-

Now she's really hunting cocaine

To dull her pain

"Hey man, you workin?"

That last bag should go for ten

But he'll take a fin

He want to go in

-

"Yeah man, I'm workin."

The fiend comes and buys the rock

Runs off the block

She's on the clock

-

Will it ever stop?

The sale...the cycle

Acknowledgements

All who have shown me love, I acknowledge you...

-Nutty C-

You were the first support man and you made moves for the team. Luv!

-Cory "50" Hodges-

My brutha for life! You have shown me so much support it's too much.

You will never be forgotten and I pray one day we'll be free

And live like the kings we are.

Luv!

-Greedy G-

You are a good man and I'm sorry things went wrong for you.

Thank you for reading my other works

And telling me I can make it

Luv!

-Reece C-

You read all my other works and told me I'm better than a lot of the rest.

Thank you for showing interest, and thank you

For being my brutha beyond my craft.

Luv!

And to all the others who gave me support

Thank you and know that

I know who you are

Luv!

Passion Room

They join in the darkness of the A.M.

Under the full moon of space

Embracing one another with racing hearts and eager mouths

They are not to be

Her and he

-

For the bonds of her and his vows sealed before

The almighty says it's a sin

But cupid's arrows have struck these star crossed lovers

And fate has dealt them a troublesome blow

What are they to do?

-

Ones cannot run because on her side there are "little ones"

Who know not their mothers love for another

And do not see the folly of

Their father's unaffectionate ways

So what are they to do but part?

Part and let distance heal

-

Thus before parting, let them have coition once more

Under the stars in the stillness of the morning

Let him travel east away from West and never return

-

But do not try to forget

Because the more you try to forget

The more you remember

And the more you remember

The more likely you'll return

Just Some Thoughts

Don't you wish you could go back in time?

I do

Rewind the clock and save all the money I blew

Go back to the first crime

And stop on a dime like "Why?"

-

I would have stayed in the books

Stayed in college

Could have been something with all that knowledge

-

Wish I could go back to my first love

And be "square" instead of a thug

Because I knew before I came along

God was her world

And after I was gone

God did she love girls

-

Go back to those nights of selling crack under the street lights

And pause to reflect on life

Then stop like Mase did

Repent my sins and stop getting wasted

-

But if wish was a fifth

We'd all be drunk

But since it isn't and I'm here

I'll just continue to wish

On my bunk

The Way We Were

I miss Amanda

Plain and simple

I miss her smile

I miss her dimples

-

I want to hold her tight

With my face in her neck

Breathing in her essence

Just for one sec

-

I miss Mandy

Sad, but true

I miss her saying

"I love you."

-

I want to kiss her palms

And each finger tip

All the way up

To her strawberry lips

-

I want to tilt her head back gently

By the chin

Some may have seen a "4"

But I saw a "10"

I wish she'd tell me she wanted me again

-

I miss Amanda

And what we had

I want "us" back

Oh so bad

-

My whole being yearns

Until "we" return

But until that moment

My heart still burns

-

Liquids mirror my souls in half

I have regrets

Regrets I have

Breathe These Words

As I walk through this world like a ghost

I contemplate the meaning of my life

Adding and subtracting the motive that lead me down this path

-

My mind washes over like a bath

On a supernatural sabbatical dissecting the things that we were

Instead of the actual

You see...

-

I was lost

I was a fool to think I was cool

Carrying a tool to school

And running around town laying down

With every bad girl who wanted me

-

Peddling crack rock like Pepsi

While bagging up herb pounds in hefties

Planning to be the Rick Ross the boss

Without knowing the cost

-

Lives taken by earth shattering buck shots

Making families plot

On how to pay for their loved ones last bed box

And so he fox trots

-

He fox trots the devil dances with his puppet

Strings manipulating the masses

I see these things happening

In my mind's eye

The third eye I fly

-

Even though I'm incarcerated

With love I still feel hatred

Subjected to criminals living in their mental

Basements faces

-

Come and go like sunlight summers and winter snows

My life is filled with hot and cold

Rotting souls fold

Like lawn chairs

Another Fat Boy Dream

Handmade prime sirloin burger

Seasoned just right

With garlic, pepper, and salt

Just waiting for me to bite

-

Put on a sesame seed bun topped with pepper jack cheese

Ketchup, diced onions

End guess what's on the side?

Funions!

-

Oh how I love catfish battered up good

Cornmeal, fried in good vegetable grease

Buttermilk, jalapeno, cornbread, and spaghetti

With Italian meat

-

Cheese grits with scrambled eggs and sausage links

Or just some apple jacks

That turn cold milk pink

-

Sizzled steak

A potato baked

Seven layer cake washed down

With a strawberry shake

-

Honey ham, sweet yams, and beefy burritos

Chili cheese Fritos, fried rice with pork meat diced

All the food I love to eat is far away so it seems

-

But when I close my eyes

It's no surprise

In fat boy's dreams

www.ingramcontent.com/pod-product-compliance
Lightning Source LLC
Chambersburg PA
CBHW030307030426
42337CB00012B/621